ESSENTIAL ELEMENTS

A COMPREHENSIVE BAND METHOD

by
Tom C. Rhodes • Donald Bierschenk • Tim Lautzenheiser • John Higgins

Dear Band Student,

Welcome to Essential Elements For Band! We are pleased that you have chosen to play the trumpet.
With practice and dedication, you'll enjoy a lifetime of music performance.
Best wishes for your musical success!

OF THE TRUMPET

The origins of the trumpet can be traced to ancient Egypt, Africa and Greece. These "natural" valveless trumpets were made of wood, bronze or silver. In the Middle Ages (500-1430), these instruments played only low notes. During the Renaissance era (1430-1600), they performed at many ceremonial functions. Gradually, players began to use higher notes, especially in the Baroque era (1600-1750).

Heinrich Stölzel introduced a valve trumpet in Berlin in 1814. In 1830, the B♭ Cornet was introduced in Europe. Valves made it possible to play all the notes of a chromatic scale on these two closely-related instruments.

Cornets and trumpets are the highest pitched members of the brass family. As one of the main instruments in concert band and jazz ensemble, they play melodies, harmonies and solos. Trumpets are longer than the more conically shaped cornets. In this book, we refer to the B♭ Trumpet, but the instructions apply to both instruments.

Virtually all important composers have written music for the trumpet, including J. S. Bach and W. A. Mozart. Some famous trumpet performers are Maurice André, Adolph Herseth, Doc Severinsen and Wynton Marsalis.

ISBN 978-0-7935-1259-1

HAL•LEONARD™
CORPORATION
7777 W. BLUEMOUND RD. P.O. BOX 13819 MILWAUKEE, WI 53213

00863510

D1372120

THE BASICS

Posture

Sit on the edge of your chair, and always keep your:
- Spine straight and tall
- Shoulders back and relaxed
- Feet flat on the floor

Breathing & Air Stream

Breathing is a natural thing we all do constantly. To discover the correct air stream to play your instrument:
- Place the palm of your hand near your mouth.
- Inhale deeply through the corners of your mouth, keeping your shoulders steady. Your waist should expand like a balloon.
- Slowly whisper "tah" as you gradually exhale air into your palm.

The air you feel is the air stream. It produces sound through the instrument. Your tongue is like a faucet or valve in that it releases the air stream.

Producing The Essential Tone

"Buzzing" through the mouthpiece produces your tone. The buzz is a fast vibration in the center of your lips. Embouchure (*ahm'-bah-shure*) is your mouth's position on the mouthpiece of the instrument. A good embouchure takes time and effort, so carefully follow these steps for success:

BUZZING
- Moisten your lips.
- Bring your lips together as if saying the letter "m."
- Relax your jaw to separate your upper and lower teeth.
- Form a slightly puckered smile to firm the corners of your mouth.
- Direct a full air stream through the center of your lips, creating a buzz.
- Buzz frequently without your mouthpiece.

MOUTHPIECE PLACEMENT
- Form your "buzzing" embouchure.
- Center the mouthpiece on your lips. Your teacher may suggest a slightly different mouthpiece placement.
- Take a full breath through the corners of your mouth.
- Start your buzz with the syllable "tah." Buzz through the center of your lips keeping a steady, even buzz.
- Your lips provide a cushion for the mouthpiece.

Mouthpiece Work-Outs

Like a physical work out, mouthpiece work-outs may make you dizzy and tired at first. Keep practicing, and you'll see daily improvement.

Hold the mouthpiece on the stem with your thumb and first finger. Carefully form your embouchure and take a deep breath. Begin a steady, even buzz with the syllable "tah." Your mouthpiece work-out looks like this:

For higher tones, make the opening in the center of your lips more firm. For lower tones, slightly relax the opening.

Getting It Together

Throughout this book, all instructions apply to both cornets and trumpets because they are played exactly the same way.

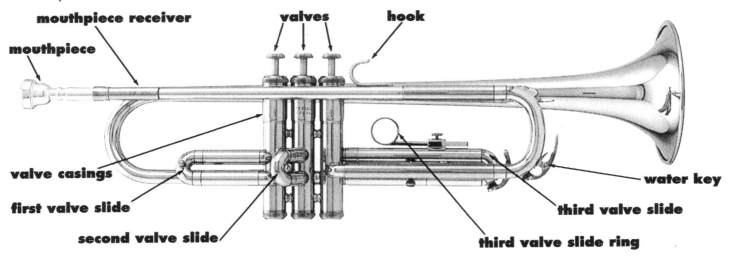

Step 1 - Put your left thumb and fingers around the valve casings and pick up the trumpet. Your left hand supports the weight of the instrument.

Step 2 - Place your left ring finger inside the ring of the third valve slide.

Step 3 - Hold the mouthpiece at the wide end with your right hand. Gently twist the mouthpiece into the mouthpiece receiver.

Step 4 - Arch your right hand to form a backwards "C." Place your thumb below the first and second valve casings. Place your little finger on top of the hook.

Step 5 - Always sit or stand tall when playing. Hold the trumpet as shown:

Let's Play!

This special exercise is just for B♭ Trumpeters and B♭ Cornetists. Place your fingers on the valves as shown: ○○○
Begin your steady, even buzz and whisper "tah" to play **G**.
Try this exercise several times.

Beat • The *Pulse* of Music

One beat = tap foot **down** on the number and **up** on the "&." Count and tap when playing or resting.

Count **1** & **2** & **3** & **4** &
Tap ↓ ↑ ↓ ↑ ↓ ↑ ↓ ↑

Fermata 🎵 Hold the note longer, or until your director tells you to release it.

Staff, Bar Lines & Measures

Bar lines divide the music staff into **measures.** The measures on this page have four beats each.

 = Music Staff

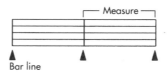

Bar line

Notes & Rests

Notes tell us how high or low to play *and* how long to play. Notes are placed on a line or space of the music staff.

Rests tell us to count silent beats.

♩ Quarter Note = 1 Beat

𝄽 Quarter Rest = 1 Silent Beat

1. COUNT AND PLAY

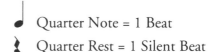

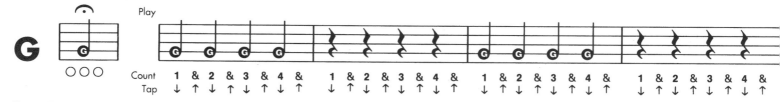

2. A NEW NOTE

3. TWO'S A TEAM

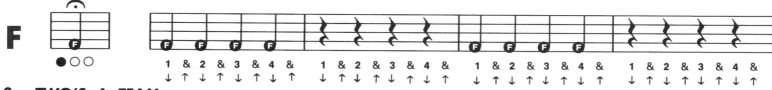

4. THE NEXT NOTE

5. DOWN AND UP

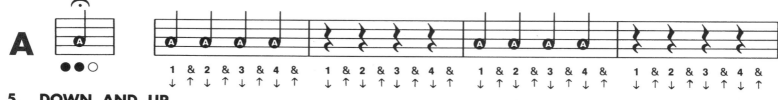

6. ROLLING ALONG

Go to next line. ▼

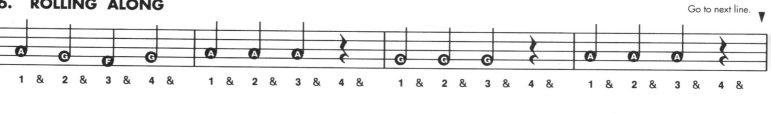

Treble Clef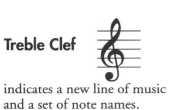

indicates a new line of music and a set of note names.

Time Signature
(Meter)

tells us how many beats are in each measure *and* what kind of note gets one beat.

$\frac{4}{4}$ – 4 beats per measure
$\frac{4}{4}$ – ♩ or ♪ gets one beat

Note Names

▲ leger line

Each line and space of the staff has a **note name** that tells us what pitch to play.

Sharp ♯ raises the note and remains in effect for the entire measure. **Flat** ♭ lowers the note and remains in effect for the entire measure. Notes not altered by sharps or flats are called **natural** notes.

NOTE FINGERING REVIEW

Double Bar

indicates the end of a piece of music.

Repeat Sign Go back to the beginning and play the line again.

7.

8. COPY CAT

9. ROLLING ALONG — Children's Song

► Practice this song on your mouthpiece only. Then, play it on your instrument.

10. FIRST FLIGHT

11. ESSENTIAL ELEMENTS QUIZ   Complete the note names before you play.

Note Names   A   F   G   A

Half Note

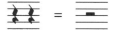

♩ ——→ = 2 Beats

1 & 2 &
↓ ↑ ↓ ↑

Half Rest

▬
1 & 2 & = 2 Silent Beats
↓ ↑ ↓ ↑

12. RHYTHM RAP   Count aloud while clapping and tapping.

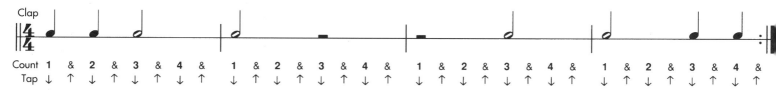

Clap

Count 1 & 2 & 3 & 4 &   1 & 2 & 3 & 4 &   1 & 2 & 3 & 4 &   1 & 2 & 3 & 4 &   1 & 2 & 3 & 4 &
Tap   ↓ ↑ ↓ ↑ ↓ ↑ ↓ ↑   ↓ ↑ ↓ ↑ ↓ ↑ ↓ ↑   ↓ ↑ ↓ ↑ ↓ ↑ ↓ ↑   ↓ ↑ ↓ ↑ ↓ ↑ ↓ ↑   ↓ ↑ ↓ ↑ ↓ ↑ ↓ ↑

13. THE HALF COUNTS

1 & 2 & 3 & 4 & 1 & 2 & 3 & 4 & 1 & 2 & 3 & 4 & 1 & 2 & 3 & 4 & 1 & 2 & 3 & 4 & 1 & 2 & 3 & 4 &

14. A NEW NOTE

E

15. MOVING AROUND

16. ANOTHER NEW NOTE

D

Breath Mark ' Take a deep breath after you play the note for full value.

17. WALKING

18. MOVING DOWN

C

19. GO TELL AUNT RHODIE

American Folk Song

► Practice this song on your mouthpiece only. Then, play it on your instrument.

20. ESSENTIAL ELEMENTS QUIZ   Write in the note names before you play.

Note Names ___ ___ ___ ___ ___ ___

29. EASY STREET

► Correct posture improves your sound. Always sit straight and tall.

30. JUMP ROPE

Theory **Harmony** Two or more different notes played or sung at the same time. A duet is a composition for two players. Practice this duet with a friend, and listen to the harmony.

31. LONDON BRIDGE - Duet

English Folk Song

32. POLLY WOLLY DOODLE

Dynamics *f* (*forte*) Play loudly. *mf* (*mezzo forte*) Play moderately loud. *p* (*piano*) Play softly.
Always use full breath support to control your tone at all dynamic levels.

33. CLAP LOUDLY

34. CLAP SOFTLY

35. SKIP TO MY LOU

American Folk Song

36. OLD MACDONALD HAD A BAND

► Practice this song on your mouthpiece only. Then, play it on your instrument.

37. ESSENTIAL ELEMENTS QUIZ Write in the note names to complete this sentence.

O U R _ _ N _ IS T H _ _ R _ _ T _ S T!

Time Signature
(Meter)

$\frac{2}{4}$ – 2 beats per measure
– ♩ or 𝄾 gets one beat

Conducting

Practice conducting this two-beat pattern.

45. RHYTHM RAP

46. OLD JOE CLARK

Count and clap before you play.

American Folk Song

> One of the world's greatest composers, **Ludwig van Beethoven** (1770-1827), became completely deaf in 1802. Although he could not hear his music like we do, he could "hear" it in his mind. The theme of his last Symphony (No. 9) is called "Ode To Joy." It was composed to the text of a poem by German writer Johann von Schiller. "Ode To Joy" was featured in concerts celebrating the reunification of Germany in 1990.

47. ODE TO JOY

Ludwig van Beethoven

48. HEY, HO! NOBODY'S HOME

Traditional

Dynamics

crescendo (cresc.) — Gradually increase volume.
decrescendo (decresc.) — Gradually decrease volume.

49. CLAP THE DYNAMICS

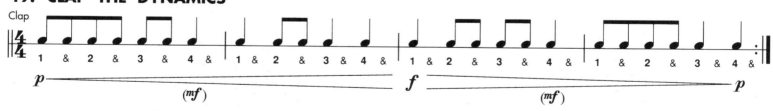

Warm-up Warming up is the proper way to begin a successful performance. After assembling your instrument, carefully set your embouchure. Start your warm-up by playing long tones in the middle register. Then play lower notes, and gradually move into higher notes using easy fingering patterns. Proper breathing and posture are always important.

50. WARM - UP CHORALE #1

51. MICHAEL ROW YOUR BOAT ASHORE - Duet

American Folk Song

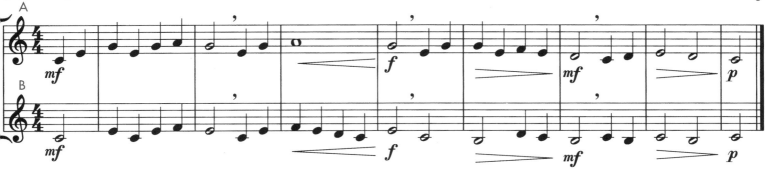

Tie 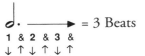 A curved line that connects notes of the **same** pitch. Play for the combined counts of the tied notes.

52. FIT TO BE TIED

▲ Hold these tied notes for 2 beats.

53. ALOUETTE

French Folk Song

▲ Hold these tied notes for 3 beats.

Dotted Half Note

 = 3 Beats

1 & 2 & 3 &
↓ ↑ ↓ ↑ ↓ ↑

♩. ◄ Dot
A dot adds half the value of the note.

2 beats + 1 beat = 3 beats

54. RETURN TO ALOUETTE'S PLACE

French Folk Song

American composer **Stephen Collins Foster** (1826-1864) wrote 189 songs, many of which became classic American folk songs. Most of Foster's songs were published shortly before the American Civil War (1860-1865). His works include "Oh, Susanna," "My Old Kentucky Home" and "Camptown Races."

55. CAMPTOWN RACES

Stephen Collins Foster

Tempo The speed of music. Tempo markings are usually written in Italian and are found above the staff.

Andante — Slow walking tempo   **Moderato** — Moderate tempo   **Allegro** — Fast bright tempo

56. ESSENTIAL ELEMENTS QUIZ

Moderato

Where is beat 4? ▲

Time Signature (Meter) **3** – 3 beats per measure
4 – ♩ or 𝄽 gets one beat

Conducting Practice conducting this three-beat pattern.

57. RHYTHM RAP

Clap

Count 1 & 2 & 3 & ...
Tap ↓ ↑ ↓ ↑ ↓ ↑ ...

58. A MINI WALTZ
Count and clap before you play.

Moderato

► Always use a full air stream. Keep your right little finger on top of the ring.

History Norwegian composer **Edvard Grieg** (1843-1907) wrote *Peer Gynt Suite* in 1875 for a play by Henrik Ibsen. Music used in plays, films, radio and television is called **incidental music.** *Peer Gynt Suite* was written the year before the telephone was invented by Alexander Graham Bell. "Morning" is a melody from the first movement of the *Peer Gynt Suite*.

59. MORNING
Edvard Grieg

Accent ♩ or ⪈ Emphasize the note.

60. ACCENT YOUR TALENT

Clap

History **Latin American music** combines the folk music from South and Central America, the Caribbean Islands, American Indian, African, Spanish and Portuguese cultures. In this diverse music, melodies feature a lively accompaniment by drums, maracas and claves. Latin American music continues to influence jazz, classical and popular styles of music. This melody, also known as *Chiapanecas*, is a popular children's dance and game song in Latin American countries.

61. MEXICAN CLAPPING SONG
Latin American Folk Song

62. RISING MUFFINS

B♭ B - flat

▲ Remember, the ♭ applies to all B's in this measure.

63. ESSENTIAL ELEMENTS QUIZ - RUSSIAN DANCE

1st and 2nd Endings  Play the 1st ending the 1st time through. Then, repeat the same section of music, skip the 1st ending and play the 2nd ending.

64. CIRCUS WALTZ

65. HATIKVAH

Hebrew Folk Song

History **Japanese folk music** has origins in ancient China. "Sakura, Sakura" was written for the koto, a 13-string instrument that is over 4000 years old. The unique sound of this ancient Japanese song results from the pentatonic, or five-note sequence used in this tonal system.

66. SAKURA, SAKURA - Full Band Arrangement (Song of the Blooming Cherry Tree)

Japanese Folk Song
Arr. by John Higgins

67. THE BIG AIR STREAM

68. JOLLY OLD ST. NICK - Duet

69. TECHNIQUE TRAX

Andante

► Keep your fingers on top of the valves, arched naturally.

![Theory] **Theme and Variations** A musical form where a theme is followed by variations, or different versions, of the theme. A theme is usually a short melody.

70. VARIATIONS ON A FAMILIAR THEME

Theme   Variation 1

Variation 2

▲ Play B - naturals.

D.C. al Fine   Play until you see the *D.C. al Fine*. Then, go back to the beginning and play until you see *Fine* (fee'-nay). *D.C.* is the Latin abbreviation for *Da Capo*, or return to the beginning. *Fine* is Latin for "the finish."

71. BANANA BOAT SONG

Latin American Folk Song

Moderato   **Fine**

D.C. al Fine

72. THE LITTLE MUSIC BOX

F♯ F - sharp   **Moderato**

▲ Remember, the ♯ applies to all F's in the measure.

![History] **Black American spirituals** originated in the 1700's. As one of the largest categories of true American folk music, these melodies were sung and passed on for generations without being written down. Black and white people worked together to publish the first spiritual collection in 1867, four years after The Emancipation Proclamation was signed into law. "What A Morning" is a famous Black American spiritual.

73. ESSENTIAL ELEMENTS QUIZ - WHAT A MORNING

Black American Spiritual

Andante   **Fine**

D.C. al Fine

Slur A curved line that connects notes of **different** pitches. Tongue only the first note of each group of notes connected by a slur.

74. SMOOTH OPERATOR

p ▲ Slur 2 notes. Tongue the first note. Play the next note without tonguing.

75. GLIDING ALONG

mf ▲ Slur 4 notes. Tongue only the first note of notes connected by a slur.

History **Ragtime** is an American music style (1896-1918) that was popular before World War I. It uses early forms of jazz rhythms. Scott Joplin wrote many ragtime piano pieces. The trombones will now learn a *glissando*, a technique used in ragtime and other styles of music.

76. TROMBONE RAG

Allegro

f

Phrases Musical sentences that are usually 2 or 4 measures long. Try to play phrases in one breath.

77. THE COLD WIND

B

B-natural ○●○

Multiple Measures Rest

The large number tells you how many measures to count and rest. Count each measure in sequence: **1 2 3 4 | 2 2 3 4**

78. SATIN LATIN

mf

▲ Play all F's as F#'s and all B's as B - naturals.

mf

History German composer **Johann Sebastian Bach** (1685-1750) wrote hundreds of choral and instrumental works. He was a master teacher, organist and famous improviser. Bach had 21 children, many of whom became famous composers. He wrote this Minuet, or dance in 3/4 time, as a piano teaching piece.

79. ESSENTIAL ELEMENTS QUIZ - MINUET - Duet

Johann Sebastian Bach

80. WARM - UP CHORALE #2 - FINLANDIA

Jean Sibelius

Andante

Repeat from beginning

p Always check the key signature.

mf *f*

mf *p*

History Austrian composer **Franz Peter Schubert** (1797-1828) was a great composer of songs, symphonies and piano works. He wrote three military marches for piano duet. "March Militaire" is the introduction and theme from one of these popular marches.

Natural Sign ♮ Cancels a flat ♭ or sharp ♯. A natural sign remains in effect for the entire measure.

81. MARCH MILITAIRE

Franz Schubert

Introduction

Theme

f

82. MY BONNIE LIES OVER THE OCEAN

Scottish Folk Song

E♭
E - flat

mf

The ♭ applies to the tied note.
Play the E♭ for 4 beats.

History **Blues** is a form of Black American folk music related to jazz. Boogie-woogie is a blues style first recorded by pianist Clarence "Pine Top" Smith in 1928, one year after Charles Lindbergh's solo flight across the Atlantic. Blues music has altered notes and is usually written in 12 bars, like "Bottom Bass Boogie."

83. BOTTOM BASS BOOGIE - Duet

A Allegro

f

B Allegro

f

A

B

Dotted Quarter Note
Eighth Note

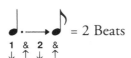 = 2 Beats

Remember, a dot adds half the value of the note.

A single eighth note has a flag on the stem.

 Flag

84. RHYTHM RAP

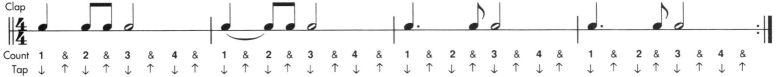

85. THE DOT ALWAYS COUNTS

86. AULD LANG SYNE

Scottish Folk Song

87. SCARBOROUGH FAIR

English Folk Song

88. ALL THROUGH THE NIGHT

History Bohemian composer **Antonin Dvořák** (1841-1904) wrote his famous **Symphony From The New World** in 1894 while living in New York. Many melodies from this work are based on American folksongs and spirituals. This is the largo (very slow tempo) theme.

89. ESSENTIAL ELEMENTS QUIZ - THEME FROM NEW WORLD SYMPHONY

Antonin Dvořák

Great musicians give encouragement to their fellow performers. Clarinetists will now learn a challenging slur pattern, called "Grenadilla Gorilla Jumps." Many clarinets are made of grenadilla wood. Brass players will learn lip slurs, a new warm-up pattern. The success of your band depends on everyone's help and patience. Let's play our best as these sections advance their musical technique.

Lip Slurs Notes that are slurred without changing valves are called lip slurs. Brass players practice lip slurs to develop a stronger embouchure and increase range. Add this pattern to your daily warm-up:

SPECIAL TRUMPET EXERCISE

90. GRENADILLA GORILLA JUMP #1

91. JUMPIN' UP AND DOWN

▲ Play B♮'s.

92. GRENADILLA GORILLA JUMP #2

93. JUMPIN' FOR JOY

Theory **Interval** The distance between two notes. Starting with "1" on the lower note, count each line and space between the notes. The number of the higher note is the distance of the interval.

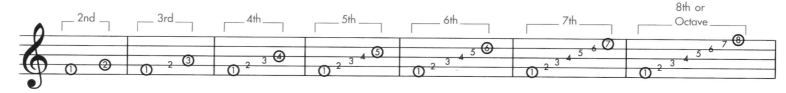

94. GRENADILLA GORILLA JUMP #3

95. JUMPIN' JACKS

96. ESSENTIAL ELEMENTS QUIZ Write in the numbers of the intervals. Remember to count **up** from the lowest note.

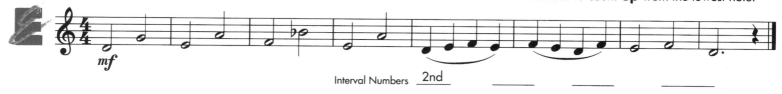

Interval Numbers   2nd

97. GRENADILLA GORILLA JUMP #4

mf

98. THREE IS THE COUNT

Draw in the bar lines before you play.

mf

99. DIXIE

Dan Emmett

▲ Play all B's as B♭'s.

f

100. GRENADILLA GORILLA JUMP #5

mf

101. TECHNIQUE TRAX

mf

Theory **Trio** A composition for three players. Practice this trio with two other players and listen for 3-part harmony.

102. KUM BAH YAH - Trio

African Spiritual

D

A **Moderato**

mf

B **Moderato**

mf

C **Moderato**

mf

A

p

B

p

C

p

103. AUSTRIAN WALTZ

Austrian Folk Song

► Higher notes are easier when you use a full air stream.

104. BOTANY BAY

Australian Folk Song

Moderato

Time Signature (Meter) C Common Time — Same as 4/4

Conducting Practice conducting this four-beat pattern.

105. TECHNIQUE TRAX

► Keep your cheeks in and direct a full air stream through your instrument.

Theory **Rounds or Canons** A musical form where performers play or sing the same melody and enter at different times. This is called **counterpoint**, a type of harmony. Divide into groups, and play "Kookaburra" as a 2-part round.

106. KOOKABURRA - Round

By Marion Sinclair

Copyright © 1934 (Renewed) by Larrikin Music Publishing Pty Ltd. for the World
Reprinted by Permission of Music Sales Corporation throughout the U.S. and Canada

107. UP ON THE HOUSETOP - Duet

B.R. Hanby

A Allegro

B Allegro

Theory **Meter Change** Occasionally, the meter (time signature) changes in music. Watch for meter changes and count carefully.

108. ESSENTIAL ELEMENTS QUIZ - METER MANIA #1 Count and clap before playing. Can you conduct this?

109. EASY JUMPS

110. TECHNIQUE TRAX

▲ Always check the key signature.

111. GERMAN FOLK SONG

Repeat Sign 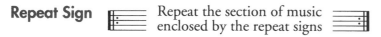 Repeat the section of music enclosed by the repeat signs

112. WHEN THE SAINTS GO MARCHIN' IN

American Folk Song

113. LOWLAND GORILLA WALK

114. SMOOTH SAILING

115. MORE EASY JUMPS

▲ Play B♮'s.

116. CAREFUL CLARINET COVER

Rehearsal Numbers [5] Measure numbers in squares above the staff.

117. SCHOOL SPIRIT - Full Band Arrangement

W. T. Purdy
Arr. by John Higgins

Austrian composer **Franz Josef Haydn** (1732-1809) wrote 104 symphonies. Many of these works had nicknames, including "The Surprise" Symphony No. 94. In the soft second movement, Haydn deliberately added sudden loud dynamics to wake up an often-sleepy audience. Here is that famous theme. Pay special attention to the dynamics.

118. SURPRISE SYMPHONY THEME

Franz Josef Haydn

119. YOU ARE A PERCUSSIONIST

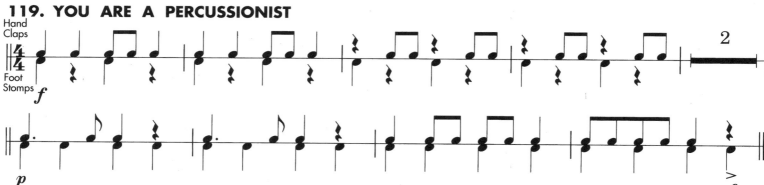

120. ESSENTIAL ELEMENTS QUIZ - THE STREETS OF LAREDO

American Folk Song

Write in the note names before you play.

Note Names ___ ___ ___ ___ ___ ___ ___ ___ ___ ___ ___ ___

Theory **Scale** A sequence of notes in ascending or descending order. The first and last notes of most scales are the same as the name of the scale. The interval between these two notes is called an **octave**.

121. CONCERT B♭ SCALE   (Your C Scale)   Memorize this exercise.

► Practice at all dynamic levels.

Tuning Musicians need to match pitches to play "in tune." We all play the same pitch to check our tuning. A common band tuning note is called **Concert B♭**.

To play Concert B♭ play your written **C:** If you are **above** the pitch (sharp), **pull** the tuning slide **out** slightly.
(Your instrument sounds a B♭ when you play your written C.) If you are **below** the pitch (flat), **push** the tuning slide **in** slightly.

Theory **Arpeggio** A sequence of notes from any scale. Your first arpeggio uses the 1st, 3rd, 5th and 8th steps from the Concert B♭ scale.

122. CONCERT B♭ SCALE AND ARPEGGIO   (Your C Scale)   Memorize this exercise.

► Practice at all dynamic levels.
► Practice this exercise on your mouthpiece only. Then, play it on your instrument.

Soli Entire section plays or is featured. In "Carnival Of Venice," listen and name the sections that play the *Soli* at each rehearsal number.

123. CARNIVAL OF VENICE - Full Band Arrangement

Julius Benedict
Arr. by John Higgins

124. A DANCING MELODY

Moderato

American composer and conductor **John Philip Sousa** (1854-1932) wrote 136 marches. Known as "The March King," Sousa wrote *The Stars And Stripes Forever, Semper Fidelis, The Washington Post* and many other patriotic pieces. Sousa's band performed all over the country, and his fame helped boost the popularity of bands in America. Here is a melody from his famous *El Capitan* operetta and march.

125. EL CAPITAN

John Philip Sousa

Allegro

▲ Play B♮'s.

"O Canada," formerly known as "National Song," was first performed in French Canada during 1880. Robert Stanley Weir translated the English version in 1908. It was officially adopted as the national anthem of Canada in 1980, one hundred years after its premier.

126. O CANADA

Calixa Lavallee,
l'Hon. Judge Routhier
and Justice R.S.Weir

Maestoso (Majestically)

127. ESSENTIAL ELEMENTS QUIZ - METER MANIA #2   Count and clap before playing. Can you conduct this?

Theory · **Enharmonics** Notes that are written differently but sound the same and are played with the same fingerings. Your fingering chart (pgs. 30-31) shows the enharmonic notes and fingerings for your instrument.

128. SNAKE CHARMER

A♭ / G♯
A-flat   G-sharp

Enharmonic notes. Use the same fingering.

129. CLOSE ENCOUNTERS

E♭ / D♯
E-flat   D-sharp

Enharmonic notes. Use the same fingering.

130. NOTES IN DISGUISE

Theory · **Chromatics** Notes that are altered with sharps, flats and naturals. The smallest distance between two notes is called a **half-step**. A scale made up of consecutive half-steps is called a **chromatic scale**.

131. HALF - STEPPIN'

History · French composer **Camille Saint-Saëns** (1835-1921) wrote many operas, suites, symphonies and chamber works. His famous opera *Samson et Delila* was written in 1877, the same year that Thomas Edison invented the phonograph. "Egyptian Dance" is one of the main opera themes from *Samson et Delila*.

132. EGYPTIAN DANCE

Camille Saint- Saëns

26

History

Russian composer **Peter Illyich Tchaikovsky** (1840-1893) wrote 6 symphonies, 3 ballets and hundreds of other works. He was a master at writing popular melodies. His *1812 Overture* and this famous melody from *Capriccio Italien* were both written in 1880, one year after Thomas Edison invented an improved light bulb.

133. CAPRICCIO ITALIEN

Peter I. Tchaikovsky

134. AMERICAN PATROL

F.W. Meacham

135. WAYFARING STRANGER

Black American Spiritual

136. ESSENTIAL ELEMENTS QUIZ - CONCERT B♭ SCALE COUNTING CONQUEST

Performing for an audience is an exciting part of being involved in music. This solo is based on Johannes Brahms' **Symphony No. 1 in C Minor, Op. 68.** Brahms was a German composer who lived from 1833-1897. He completed his first symphony in 1876, the same year that Alexander Graham Bell invented the telephone. You and a piano accompanist can perform for the band, your school and at other occasions.

137. THEME - FROM SYMPHONY NO. 1 - Solo (E♭ Concert version)

Johannes Brahms
Arr. by John Higgins

138. AMERICA THE BEAUTIFUL - Full Band Arrangement

Samuel A. Ward
Arr. by John Higgins

139. LA CUCARACHA - Full Band Arrangement

Latin American Folk Song
Arr. by John Higgins

140. THEME FROM 1812 OVERTURE - Full Band Arrangement

Peter I. Tchaikovsky
Arr. by John Higgins

B♭ TRUMPET/B♭ CORNET FINGERING CHART

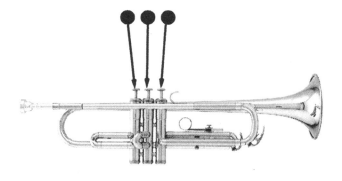

B♭ Trumpet

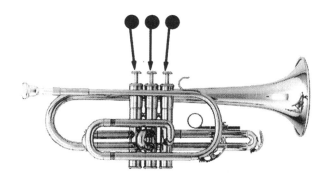

B♭ Cornet

 = UP   = PRESSED DOWN

Instruments courtesy of
Yamaha Corporation of America
Band and Orchestral Division.

Take Special Care

Before putting your instrument back in its case after playing, do the following:
- Use the water key to empty water from the instrument. Blow air through it..
- Remove the mouthpiece. Wash your mouthpiece with warm tap water once per week. Dry thoroughly.
- Wipe the instrument off with a clean soft cloth. Return the instrument to its case.

Trumpet valves occasionally need oiling. To oil your trumpet valves, simply:
- Unscrew the valve at the top of the casing.
- Lift the valve half-way out of the casing.
- Apply a few drops of oil to the exposed valve.
- Carefully return the valve to the casing. When properly inserted, the top of the valve should screw back into place.
- Be sure to grease the slides regularly. Your director will recommend valve oil and slide grease, and will help you apply them when necessary.

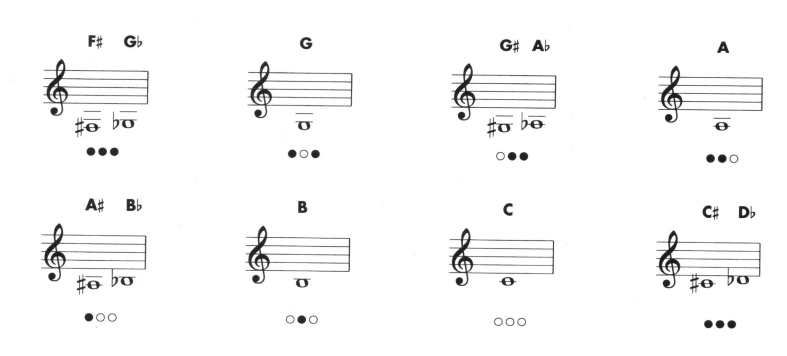

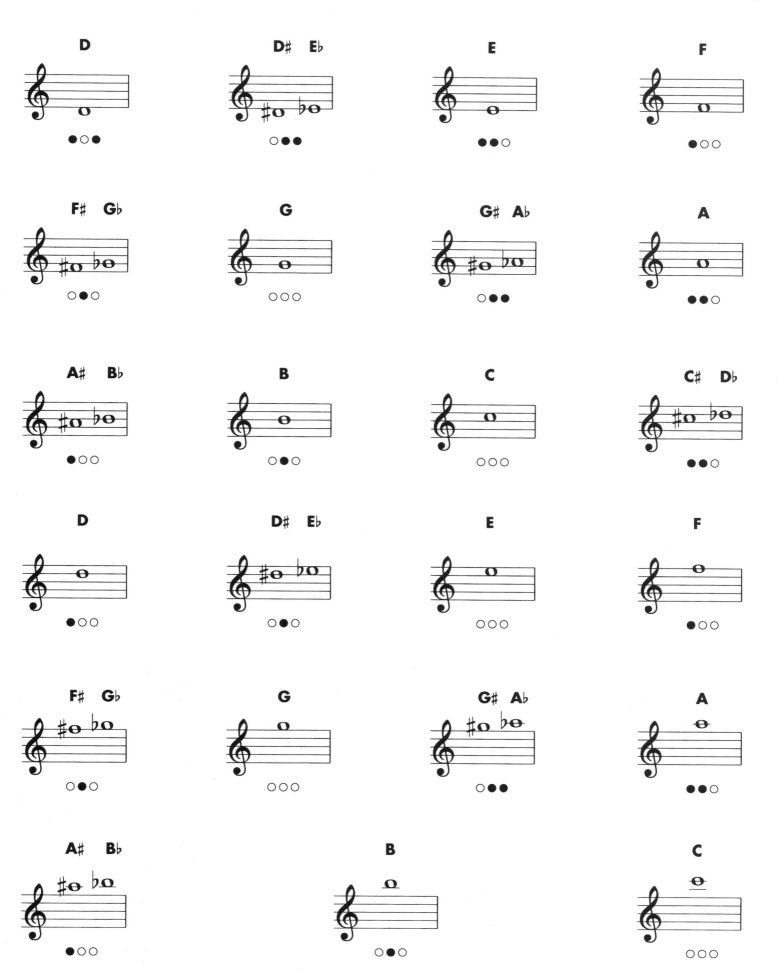

GLOSSARY

Essential Element	Definition
Accent	Emphasize the note.
Allegro	Fast bright tempo.
Andante	Slow walking tempo.
Arpeggio	A sequence of notes from any scale.
Bach, Johann Sebastian	German composer (1685-1750).
Bar Lines	Divide the music staff into measures.
Bass Clef	"F" clef used by trbs., bar, bsn. and tuba.
Beat	The pulse of music.
Beethoven, Ludwig van	German composer (1770-1827).
Black American Spirituals	Music style originating in the 1700's.
Blues	Music form and style related to jazz.
Breath Mark	Take a deep breath after playing the note full value.
Chromatics	Notes that are altered with sharps, flats and naturals.
Chromatic Scale	Sequence of notes in half-steps.
Common Time	Another way to write $\frac{4}{4}$.
Concert Bb	Band tuning note.
Crescendo	Gradually increase volume.
D.C. al Fine	*Da Capo al Fine* - Play until *D.C. al Fine*. Go back to the beginning and play until *Fine*.
Decrescendo	Gradually decrease volume.
Dotted Note	The dot adds half the value of the note.
Double Bar	Indicates the end of a piece of music.
Duet	Composition for two players.
Dvořák, Antonin	Bohemian composer (1841-1904).
Dynamics	The volume of music.
Embouchure	Position of your mouth on the mouthpiece.
Enharmonics	Notes that are written differently but sound the same.
Fermata	Hold the note longer, or until your director tells you to release it.
1st and 2nd Endings	Play the 1st ending the 1st time through. Then, repeat the same music skip the 1st ending and play the 2nd.
Flat	Lowers the note and remains in effect the entire measure.
forte	Play loudly.
Foster, Stephen Collins	American composer (1826-1864).
Glissando *gliss.*	Slide from one note to another.
Grieg, Edvard	Norwegian composer (1843-1907).
Half-step	The smallest distance between two notes.
Harmony	Two or more different notes played or sung at the same time.
Haydn, Franz Josef	Austrian composer (1732-1809).
Interval	The numerical distance between two notes.
Japanese Folk Music	Music from Japan.
Key Signature	Flats or sharps next to the clef that apply to entire piece.
Largo	Very slow tempo.
Latin American Music	Music from Latin American cultures.
Leger Lines	Adds notes outside of the music staff.

Essential Element	Definition
Lip Slurs	Brass instrument exercise of playing slurred notes without changing valves.
Measure	A segment of music divided by bar lines.
Meter Change	A meter (time signature) change in music.
mezzo forte	Play moderately loud.
Moderato	Moderate tempo.
Mozart, Wolfgang Amadeus	Austrian composer (1756-1791).
Multiple Measures Rest	The number indicates how many measures to count and rest.
Music Staff	Lines and spaces where notes are placed.
Natural Sign	Cancels a flat b or sharp # in the measure.
Notes	Tell us how high or low to play *and* how long to play.
Phrases	Musical sentences that are usually 2 or 4 measures long.
piano	Play softly.
Pick-up Notes	Note or notes that come before the first full measure.
Rehearsal Numbers	Measure numbers in squares above the staff.
Repeat Sign	Go back to the beginning and play again.
	Repeat the section of music enclosed by repeat signs.
Ragtime	Music style popular from 1896-1918.
Rests	Silent beats of music.
Rossini, Gioachino	Italian composer (1792-1868).
Round or Canon	Musical form where instruments play the same melody entering at different times.
Saint-Saëns, Camille	French composer (1835-1921).
Scale	Sequence of notes in ascending or descending order.
Schubert, Franz Peter	Austrian composer (1797-1828).
Sharp #	Raises the note and remains in effect the entire measure.
Slur	A curved line that connects notes of different pitches.
Soli	Entire section plays or is featured.
Sousa, John Philip	American composer (1854-1932).
Tchaikovsky, Peter Illyich	Russian composer (1840-1893).
Tempo	The speed of music.
Theme and Variations	Musical form where a theme is followed by variations of the theme.
Tie	A curved line that connects notes of the same pitch.
Time Signature (Meter)	Tells how many beats are in each measure and what kind of note gets one beat.
Treble Clef	"G" clef used by fls., ob., clar., sax. and tpt.
Trio	Composition for three players.
Tuning	Matching pitches, listening and instrument adjusting.